Genoa
Venice
Mediterranean Sea
Black Sea
Trebizond
Mt Ararat
Acre
Jerusalem
Persia
Kerman
Arabia
Indian Ocean
India
Ceylon

The journeys of

MARCO POLO

The Silk Road

SIA

Tibet

China

Burma

Malaya

Sumatra

Java

Shangtu

Peking

Japan

OXFORD ENGLISH PICTURE READERS

Grade One

MARCO POLO

OXFORD ENGLISH PICTURE READERS
COLOUR EDITION

MARCO POLO

by ANTHONY TOYNE

Illustrated by TERENCE DALLEY

OXFORD UNIVERSITY PRESS

Oxford University Press, Walton Street, Oxford OX2 6DP

Oxford   New York   Toronto
Delhi   Bombay   Calcutta   Madras   Karachi
Petaling Jaya   Singapore   Hong Kong   Tokyo
Nairobi   Dar es Salaam   Cape Town
Melbourne   Auckland

and associated companies in
Berlin   Ibadan

© *Oxford University Press 1974*
First colour edition 1975
Eleventh impression 1989

Oxford English and the *Oxford English logo* are trade marks of
Oxford University Press

ISBN   0   19   581159   3

Printed in Hong Kong

Contents

1. Marco's father goes to China

This is Venice. Venice is built on several islands in the sea. There are not many streets in Venice, but there are a lot of canals. Ships come to Venice from all over the world.

The boy in the picture is Marco Polo, and he lived in Venice a long time ago. When he was six years old his father said to him, 'Marco, I am going away.'

'Where are you going, Father?' asked Marco.

'I am going to Asia with your uncle, and we shall be away for a long time,' his father replied. 'You must be a good boy, and help your mother.'

Marco's father and uncle were merchants. They bought things from Asia and sold them in Venice. They were both rich.

Marco was very lonely after his father had gone away. His mother died, and he went to live with an aunt.

He often went out in the morning and watched the ships coming in.

Several years passed, but his father and uncle did not return.

Marco's father and uncle had gone to
China, a country in Asia, and there they
met the Emperor, Kublai Khan.
Kublai Khan liked these strange men from
Venice, and he asked them many questions.

When they left China, Kublai Khan said, 'You must come back again.' He gave them a golden tablet to help them on the dangerous journey home. When they showed this tablet in towns and villages, people gave them food and horses. 'You have the Emperor's tablet,' they said. 'We will help you on your journey.'

Marco was now fifteen years old.
One day a ship came into the harbour.
Marco's father and uncle were on the
ship, and Marco ran to meet them.

2. Marco's journey begins

Marco's father stayed at home for two years. Marco was a young man by now, and he was tall and strong. 'Your uncle and I promised to return to China and visit the great Emperor, Kublai Khan, again,' said his father one day. 'Do you want to come?'

'Oh, yes, Father,' Marco replied.

'The journey will be dangerous,' said Marco's father.

'But the Emperor's city, Peking, is a wonderful place,' Marco's uncle said. 'People there wear fine silk clothes and gold jewellery. We bought some silk and gold there and we will buy a lot more. When we have sold it, we shall be rich for ever.'

So Marco's father and uncle sailed away again from Venice. It was the year 1271. This time they took Marco with them.

First they went to Jerusalem. There they got some holy oil as a present for Kublai Khan. Then they bought some food and horses.

Jerusalem

Their journey east to Peking meant travelling all the way across Asia.

'I must remember everything I see on this journey,' Marco said to himself.

They passed the snowy slopes of Mount Ararat, and people told them that Noah's Ark was still at the top.

They passed places where oil came out of the ground. Marco saw that the oil could be used for lighting lamps.

'One day,' Marco said, 'I shall write a book about this journey.'

Marco travelled in a caravan. A caravan is a lot of people riding together for safety, with servants, horses, camels, and carts.
The caravan travelled about twenty miles a day. It crossed windy deserts and passed big, dry mountains.

3. The robbers of Kerman

After a few weeks the caravan arrived in Persia.

Here there were cities with beautiful gardens, flowers, and lovely trees. Marco enjoyed eating their big, strange fruits.

The people of the city of Kerman made swords and other weapons out of steel. They also made curtains, cushions and bedspreads out of silk. On these they sewed beautiful patterns of birds and flowers. 'Kerman is on the great Silk Road to China,' Marco's uncle said. 'The Chinese bring silk and gold to Europe along the Silk Road. The Emperor makes the road safe for all merchants travelling to and from Europe.'

The caravan followed the Silk Road. The travellers climbed a high mountain pass and then came down into a hot, dusty plain.

'There are robbers on this plain,' one man said.

Suddenly there was a dust storm. The dust went into Marco's eyes and mouth. Everything was dark. At that moment there was a terrible shout. Marco heard the sound of galloping horses.

'The robbers!' his uncle shouted. 'Follow me!'

Marco and his father and uncle rode close to each other. They knocked down one group of robbers, and then galloped to the safety of the nearest village.

They heard the noise of fighting and the screams of the other travellers on the road behind them.

'Stop!' Marco cried. 'We must go back and help.'

'No,' his uncle replied. 'We cannot help them.'

'Look,' said his father. 'Here is an empty house. We must hide here until morning.'

4. The Silk Road

None of the other people in the caravan
escaped. All of them were killed or captured by the robbers. But Marco, his
father, and his uncle met some more
merchants and continued on the Silk
Road to China.

Marco saw many strange things on the way. He saw camels with two humps, and a lot of big sheep with long, curling horns. One day he even saw some elephants. They travelled through Asia for over a year, often without water, and Marco was ill.

But they found a plain at the top of a mountain. It was covered with grass and trees. There were streams of sparkling water full of fish.

In this place, Marco soon got well again.

Then they travelled about ten miles a day through very high mountains. It was very cold.

They could not cook, because the water did not boil.

Marco's uncle said, 'I wish we had some hot soup. I am very hungry.'

Then they came to a desert. There were snakes there, but no birds or animals. Marco saw some white bones near the road. 'They are the bones of men and horses,' his father said.

5. The Emperor, Kublai Khan

The Polos were still more than four hundred miles from Peking. They were travelling very slowly. A messenger from the Emperor came to meet them.

'Kublai Khan has heard that you are coming,' he said. 'He is waiting for you. He has sent me to bring you to his summer palace.'

The Emperor was sitting on a magnificent golden throne in his summer palace at Shangtu. He had pink cheeks and a big, black moustache. His eyes were black and very bright. A lion lay at his feet. It opened its mouth and yawned at Marco.

Marco's father and uncle knelt in front of
the Emperor on both knees. Then they
touched the ground with their foreheads.
That was the right way to greet important
people in China.

Kublai Khan smiled at them. 'Welcome
to China,' he said. Then he looked at
Marco.

'Who is this young man?' he asked.

'He is my son,' Marco's father replied,
'and he will serve you well.'

'I am glad to see your son,' said Kublai Khan. 'I will make him one of my courtiers.'

Then some other courtiers led Marco away and gave him beautiful Chinese clothes.

'How handsome I look,' Marco said to himself. 'I shall like being a courtier.'

That night the Emperor gave a big dinner party and he invited the Polos to it.

There were hundreds of courtiers and thousands of servants at the party.

The food was served on gold plates, and they drank wine out of gold cups.

Marco sat on a silk cushion and listened to the music of the Emperor's trumpeters.

His father and uncle told Kublai Khan the story of their long journey.

A courtier named Ahmad was listening. He thought, 'Why does the Emperor listen to these foreigners?' He was jealous, and he looked angrily at Marco.

6. Ahmad, the favourite courtier

At the end of the summer, Kublai Khan left Shangtu and went to his winter palace at Peking. Marco and his father and uncle went with him. Ahmad went too. He was the Emperor's favourite courtier.

Ahmad was a bad man. If he did not like someone, he told the Emperor lies about him. Then the Emperor told his servants to kill the man or to put him into prison. Kublai Khan's ministers were afraid, and they hated Ahmad. Marco was afraid of him too.

One day, two of the ministers said, 'We are going to kill Ahmad.'

They sent him a message, telling him to come alone that night to the throne room in the palace. They signed the message with the name of the Emperor's son.

Ahmad did not want to go out alone in the middle of the night. But he went because he wanted to please the Emperor's son.

It was dark when he reached the palace. The captain of the guard let him in. Ahmad went straight to the throne room. He saw a man sitting there.

He knelt down, and touched the ground with his forehead.

But it was not the Emperor's son on the throne. It was one of the ministers. As Ahmad knelt down, the other minister rushed out from behind a curtain and cut off his head.

Kublai Khan was angry when he heard what had happened. But Marco and the others told him how wicked Ahmad had been, and he forgave them all.

The Emperor said to Marco, 'You are an honest man. From now on you will be one of my most important officers.'

7. The journey to Burma

'Marco Polo,' said Kublai Khan, 'I want you to travel to the south of my empire. Go as far as Tibet and Burma. Tell me about everything you see there. It will be a dangerous journey, but some of my soldiers and servants will go with you.'

The soldiers and servants all travelled on
horses. Camels carried the tents and food.
Marco's father and uncle stayed in Peking,
so Marco said good-bye to them.

44

There is a muddy river about ten miles south of Peking.

At that time there was a long bridge across it. Marco was amazed to see this bridge. It had twenty-four arches. Huge lions carved in marble stood on each side of it. The bridge was wide enough for ten men on horses to travel across it together.

At first Marco and his men travelled through some of the richest parts of China. The roads were good, and the people were well dressed.

But after a few weeks they came near Tibet. There were fewer people here. The road climbed over high mountains and there were tigers in the forests.

Some of the forest trees were bamboos. Bamboo wood is hollow and it has air inside it. When there is a fire in a bamboo forest, this air explodes with a sound like gunfire.

Marco's men put bamboo wood on their camp fires every night. It burned with a loud noise: BANG! POP! BANG! The noise frightened the tigers away.

Near Burma, Marco saw some crocodiles in a river. A man told him, 'The crocodiles come out of the river at night. They look for baby tigers. Sometimes a mother tiger finds a crocodile near her home. Then there is a terrible battle.'

Once, Marco saw a tiger and a crocodile fighting. The crocodile won.

8. The journey to India

Marco Polo went back to China and told the Emperor everything he had seen. Kublai Khan was very pleased.
'Now you must go to Ceylon,' he said. 'The king there has a jewel—a huge ruby. I want you to buy it for me.'

The journey to Ceylon was by sea. Kublai Khan gave Marco ships and men. First Marco's ships sailed to Malaya. Then they were blown by a storm to the island of Sumatra.

Here Marco and his men built wooden forts. Then they dug ditches round them, because there were cannibals on the island. Cannibals are men who eat other men.

They stayed on Sumatra for five months.
Then they sailed to Ceylon.
But the king of Ceylon would not sell
Marco his ruby. He held it in his hand
and touched his eyes and mouth with it.
It was dark red, and it shone brightly.
'This is a magic jewel,' he said. 'It gives
health and long life to its owner. I will not
sell it.'

Marco was sad. He said, 'I shall go to India for jewels instead.'

On the south coast of India he found some fishermen. 'We are fishing for pearls,' they said. They dived into the sea from little boats. They swam to the bottom of the sea bed and they came up with oysters.

When they opened the oyster shells with their sharp knives, Marco saw pearls in some of them.

Marco saw many interesting things in India. He saw holy men, called yogis.
Yogis live very simply. They will not kill anything, not even a fly. They eat very little, and yet some of them live for more than a hundred years.

In those days, people in Europe were very dirty. Some of Marco's friends never washed themselves. But in India people washed themselves all over before every meal.

Marco watched the Indians drinking water. They did not touch the cup with their lips. Instead they held the cup above their heads and poured the water into their mouths.

9. The voyage home

Marco Polo had now been in Asia for nearly twenty years. He was almost forty years old. He had seen more of the world than any other man.

His father and uncle were old men now, and they were very rich. One day they said to Kublai Khan, 'We would like to go home to Venice.' 'Very well,' said the Emperor. 'But you must take a princess from my court with you. She is going to marry the king of Persia.'

Marco's uncle was busy. He was sewing
jewels into the linings of their coats.

'We shall be rich for ever,' he said.

Kublai Khan gave them more jewels. He
also gave them fourteen ships.

Marco and his father and uncle got into
one of the ships. The princess went with
them.

The wind was blowing, and the fourteen ships sailed slowly out of the harbour. After three months they reached Java and the Indian Ocean. Eighteen months later they reached the Persian coast.

The princess had grown fond of Marco Polo during this long time. She wept when she said good-bye. Marco was sorry for her. But he was in a hurry. He wanted to get back to Venice quickly.

The Polos left the Emperor's ships in Persia. They went in a caravan from Persia to Trebizond on the Black Sea. From Trebizond they sailed the last part of the journey home.
It was 1295. They had been away for twenty-four years.

At last, they saw the roofs of the beautiful palaces and churches of Venice appear one day above the horizon. Ships with coloured sails lay in the harbour, and small boats moved along the canals.

'Father!' Marco shouted excitedly. 'Look! There is our house. We are home!'

10. Marco's book

But Marco did not stay at home for long. A war started between Venice and another city called Genoa. There was a battle between the ships of Venice and the ships of Genoa. Marco was on one of the Venetian ships. It was attacked by a Genoese ship and it was captured.

Marco was taken prisoner. He was taken to Genoa and put into prison.

Time passed slowly in prison. But Marco was cheerful. Every day he told the other prisoners stories about his travels.

The prisoners were astonished when Marco told them about the countries of Asia. One of the prisoners started to write the stories down in a book.

When Marco left prison, three years later, the book was finished.

Marco took the book back to Venice. People read it, but they said, 'This book cannot be true.'

Then Marco's father and uncle died. Now he was rich, but he did not leave Venice again.

He married, and had three daughters.

His daughters grew up and married. Soon Marco had grandchildren too.

When Marco was an old man, he was ill. Some of his friends came to see him in bed. 'Now tell us that your book is not true,' they said.

'No!' said Marco. 'Everything in my book is true. I went to all those countries, and I saw all those strange and wonderful things. It is all true.'

Genoa

Venice

Mediterranean Sea

Black Sea

Trebizond

Mt. Ararat

Acre

Jerusalem

Persia

Kerman

Arabia

Indian Ocean

India

Ceylon

The journeys of

A

MARCO POLO

The Silk Road

S I A

Tibet

China

Burma

Malaya

Sumatra

Java

Shangtu

Peking

Japan